BUSY TIMES

My Busy Week

Clare Hibbert

Illustrated by Silvia Raga

Evans

Published by Evans Brothers Limited
2A Portman Mansions, Chiltern Street, London W1U 6NR

© Evans Brothers Limited 2011
Concept devised for Evans Brothers by Clare Hibbert

Educational consultants: Sue Palmer, Josephine Hussey
Editor: Clare Hibbert
Designer: Sandra Perry
Illustrator: Silvia Raga (Milan Illustration Agency)

British Library Cataloguing in Publication Data

Hibbert, Clare, 1970-
My busy week. -- (Busy times)
1. Week--Juvenile literature. 2. Time management--Juvenile literature.
I. Title II. Series
529.2-dc22

ISBN-13: 9780237542641

Printed in China by New Era Printing Company Ltd.

The website addresses on page 22 are correct at the time of going to print but the publisher cannot be held responsible for changes to website addresses or content.

Contents

On Monday morning my class visits the library. I find a book to take home.

At the library

shelf

4

Monday afternoons
BABY RHYME TIME

rug

books

Gran always does her washing on Monday.

5

On Tuesday I go swimming after school. I'm in the beginners' class.

Swimming

instructor

swimming hat

6

goggles

float

Every Tuesday, my friend Ahmed goes to the mosque after school.

7

On Wednesday I get a gold star. It's for helping to tidy away all the toys.

Helping teacher

brick

box

CLATTER

8

table

Wednesday's the day the recycling truck comes to our road.

9

On Thursday I have a check-up at the dentist's. She gives me a sticker.

At the dentist's

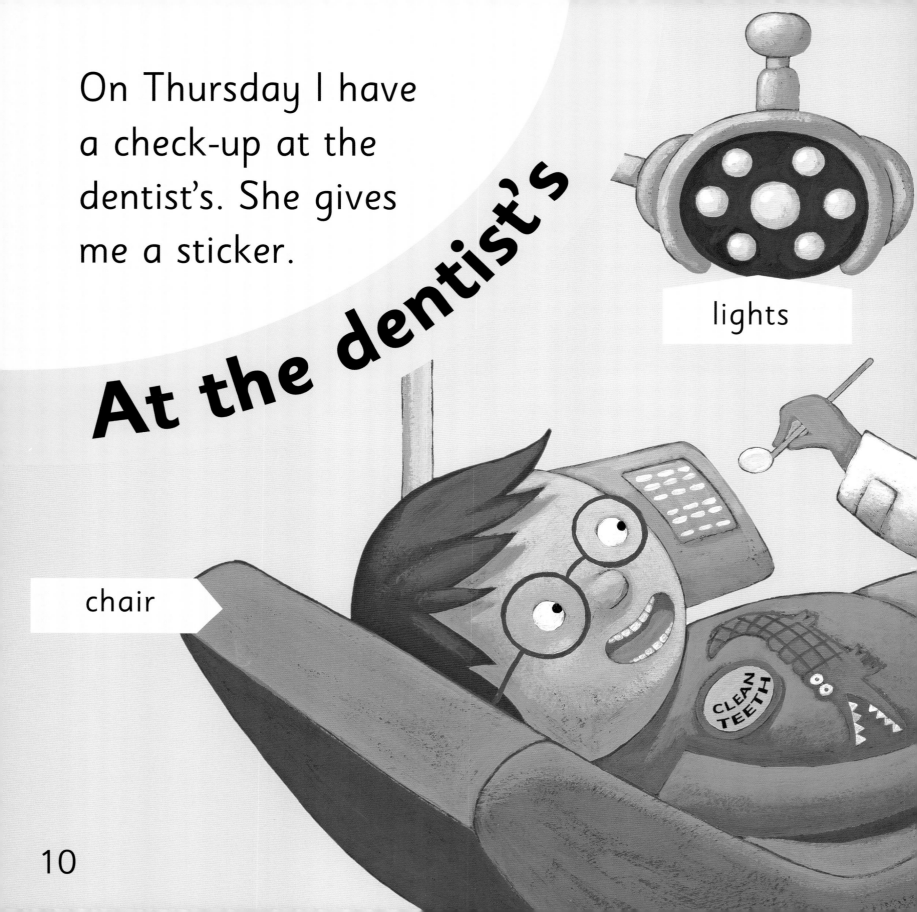

lights

chair

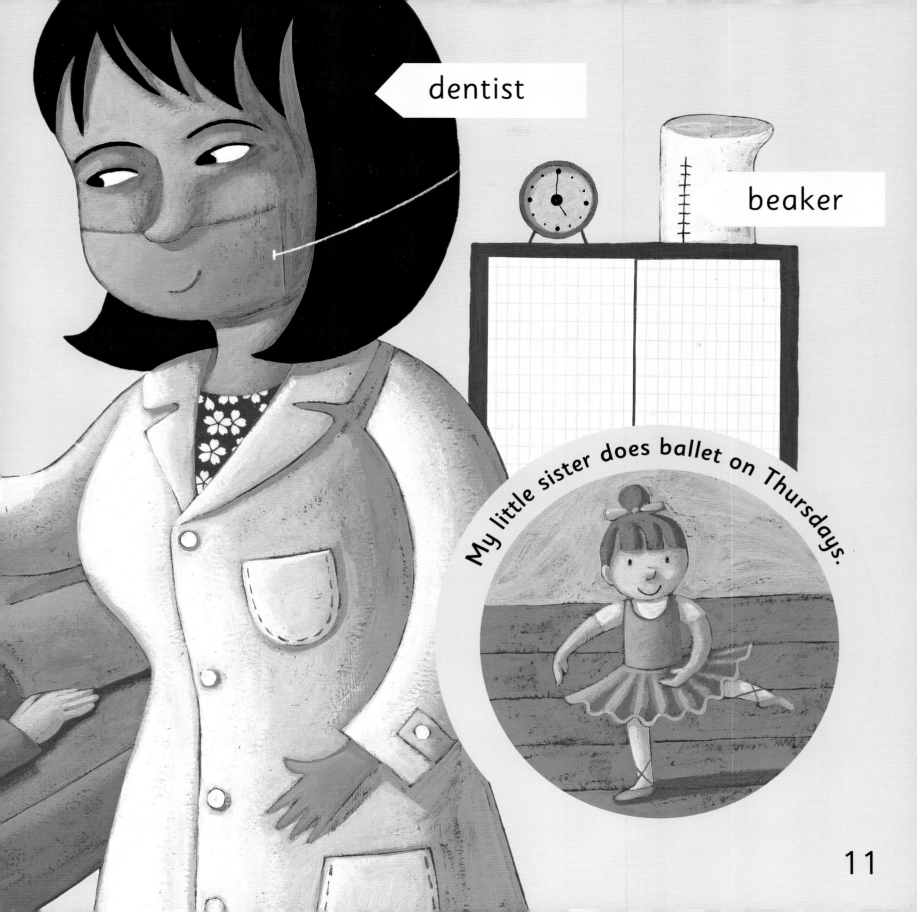

dentist

beaker

My little sister does ballet on Thursdays.

11

On Friday we make popcorn. Then we snuggle up to watch a DVD.

Home movie

sofa

blanket

popcorn

Restaurants and cafés are busy on Friday nights.

13

On Saturday it's my turn to clean out the guinea pigs. Count how many we have!

Pet care

hay

water

run

MUNCH, MUNCH

hay

bowl

My brother goes to football practice on Saturday morning.

On Saturday afternoon we help Dad do the shopping. I pick the fruit.

Going shopping

apples

pears

16

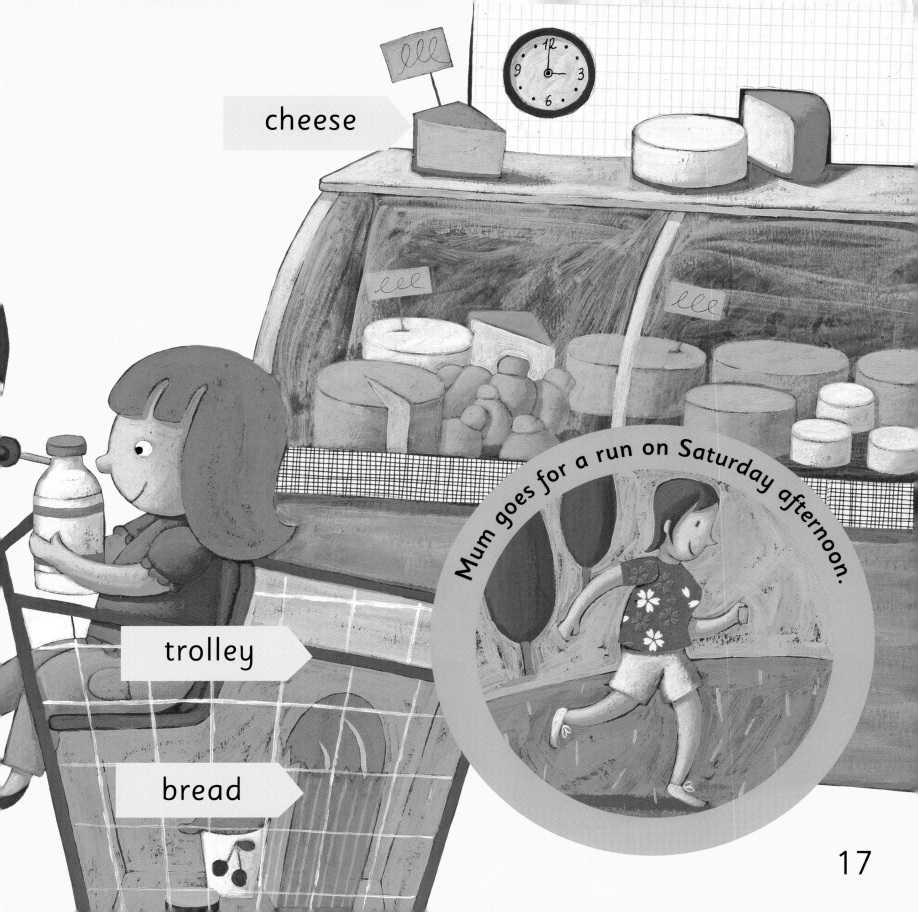

cheese

trolley

bread

Mum goes for a run on Saturday afternoon.

17

What a sunny Sunday
– perfect for going
off for a ride on
our bicycles!

Bike ride

bell

BRRRING!

saddle

wheel

WHIRR

Our neighbours go to church on Sunday morning.

19

What's my favourite time
of the whole week?
Eating roast dinner
with my family!

Sunday lunch

salt and
pepper

chicken

potatoes

20

We're visiting Grandad later. He's in hospital.

21

Notes for adults

The **Busy Times** series links in to the Early Years Foundation Stage curriculum and beyond. The series provides useful resources for exploring time in accordance with the Early Years Foundation Stage Practice Guidance from birth to five.

In today's fast-paced world, it's more important than ever to talk with young children about the passage of 'real time'. Television programmes, films and games often confuse children – for example, by using cutting techniques that telescope time passing.

The series supports young children as they begin to grasp the complex concept of time. It looks at how we mark specific moments, and how children can come to predict the order of routine events. Although children do not tell the time at this stage, they will enjoy hunting for the hidden clocks and watches.

In order to introduce the passing of time in an age-appropriate way, every spread in the **Busy Times** books illustrates a moment in a child's day, week, year or life.

As you explore the books together, you can use the pages to link in with the specifics of the child reader's life. Discuss what he or she does at those particular times. Which settings are familiar favourites? Which activities are new or unfamiliar?

Each spread also has a unique 'Window on the World' feature. Through this, children can glimpse something else happening at the same time as the main action on the spread – another, concurrent event. The window is really useful for broadening children's perspective, helping them to understand that things go on even when they are not there.

USEFUL WEBSITES

Department for Education	www.education.gov.uk
National Literacy Trust	www.literacytrust.co.uk
Early Years resources	www.earlyyearsresources.co.uk, www.underfives.co.uk

Reading with younger children

As you read, allow quiet spaces so that children can ask questions or repeat your words. Try pausing mid-sentence so that children can predict the next word. This sort of participation gives a sense of achievement and develops early reading skills.

Follow the words with your finger. The main text in the **Busy Times** books is in Infant Sassoon, a clear, friendly font designed for children learning to read and write. The sound effects add fun and introduce readers to different levels of communication.

Take time to explore the pictures together. Ask children to find, identify, count or describe different objects – not just the hidden timepieces. Point out colours and textures. The illustration style in the **Busy Times** series is especially rich and rewarding.

Children delight in repetition; they also need to revisit complex concepts on a regular basis. Expect to share these books time after time. There is lots of scope in the pictures for many different conversations.

Use the Busy Week spreads as a springboard for extension activities:

• Practise saying the names of days of the week together. Children love to chant and it's an effective way of getting the order of the names to 'stick'.

• Asking children the questions 'What day is it today?', 'What day was it yesterday?' and 'What day will it be tomorrow?' helps them begin to understand the sequence of the days of the week.

• Enjoy the traditional rhyme 'Monday's Child is Fair of Face'. It's more fun if children find out the day they and/or their friends were born on. 'Solomon Grundy' is another rhyme that covers the days of the week.

• Help children to make a pictorial chart showing activities that they enjoy through the week. They can paint pictures or stick on relevant photos cut out from magazines.

• Encourage children to keep a weather diary for a week. Next to each day, they can add one or more simple weather symbols – for example, to represent sun, cloud, rain, wind and snow.

Index

Bb

ballet 11
bike rides 18–19
books 4–5

Dd

dentist's 10–11
DVDs 12–13

Ff

food 13, 20–21
football practice 15

Pp

pets 14–15

Ss

shopping 16–17
swimming pool 6–7